Lost in the Gaeltacht

CAROLINE LYNCH

salmonpoetry

Published in 2008 by
Salmon Poetry,
Cliffs of Moher, County Clare, Ireland
Website: www.salmonpoetry.com
Email: info@salmonpoetry.com

ISBN 978-1-903392-84-3

Cover photograph: Dug Cubie
Cover design & typesetting: Siobhán Hutson

LISTOWEL

To My Grandparents

Acknowledgements

Acknowledgements are due to the editors of the following in which some of these poems have previously appeared:

Poetry Ireland Review; The Incredible Hides in Every House, edited by Nuala Ní Dhomhnaill; *Writers Seeking Lovers* and *The Listowel Winners' Anthology 2007*.

I would like to thank the Arts Council of Ireland for the Professional Training and Development Award they awarded me in 2006 which allowed me obtain an MA in Writing from NUI, Galway.

Contents

The Match

I told the woodsman that hurleys are made of ash
and about the clash that is the cliché of all that.

By Salisbury Cathedral he explained the rules
of cricket — enthusiastic inflection, lovely round

vowels bowled across grass. Then I picked up
a sliotar on a flick of air held like a hurley

and pucked the tight wad of nothing: high, long,
over the cathedral spire's great struts of Irish oak.

The Commonplace Mother Plays Medea

She is leaving us a mystery, this commonplace
mother going where we can't follow. The muscles
in her arms are beyond us in strength. Her hands
are full. Children's faces are trapped behind
her fingers, off-stage in the dark wings of a house
while the street outside is an empty space.

Here is a view of people staring into that space,
waiting to be taken away from the commonplace.
And the view that everyone sees is of houses.
But in every house hidden rooms are muscles
knotted deep under a skin. Who can see behind
the walls of a house, or the fine skin of a hand?

Clocks in kitchens everywhere move their hands
as usual through the day. But, in the white space
between two minutes, something begins behind
the walls of one house. People of the common place,
knowing nothing of its rooms and the muscles
of an arm flexing, believe in the safety of houses

until the fourth wall falls away from the house.
Remember the superstitions of the stagehand;
a forbidden word or whistle and chaos muscles
its way into the corners of every safe space.
What thing so far beyond the commonplace
did she do to bring this monster up behind

her children, no-one nearby to call *look behind
you*, to them or her? The bricks of the house
lie about, broken remains of the commonplace
crumbled into pieces in our hands,
as if these investigations can fill the space
emptied by her final act. The heart is muscle

and hers ached. The acid in a tired muscle
stabs the flesh. She fell behind,
unable to cross the growing space
between the world and the door to her house.
She closed the door and turned her hands
over to their work, far beyond the commonplace.

No-one left in the house now can move a muscle.
No-one will clap hands to bring them out from behind
the curtains of a dark place. Their going leaves an
uncommon space.

(After the evacuation of St. Kilda
the house mouse became extinct on the island)

The Abandoned House Mouse

When they left, the rump of a great cat
settled on the roof like it was a cushion
and the silence in the house was huge.
We were alone
and we dragged ourselves, thinner and
thinner, through the cupboards emptied
of all flour, our eyes drier than crumbs.
They were gone
and we could die wherever we wanted,
mostly floating the trance of the kitchen's
earthen floor, its brown patterns gulping –
We were gone
and the house, squatting in its hollow
squinted out and saw the sea's green jaw
flexing its appetite like a winter storm.

Censors At My Table

The hear-no-evil, speak-no-evil brigade go about the
    daily business
of shredding papers assiduously with teeth, eating
    volumes of print
for breakfast, and preparing for the evening editions
    at six by slowly
rubbing their ruined stomachs gently, anti-clockwise,
    with bleach.

I crack the top of my egg, and instead of a yellow yolk
    inside there is
a little man, liquefied with grief. What will I do with this?
    I ask them
while they sit chewing columns of disaster. Their arms
    stretch across
and they dip the rippings of some scandal into him even
    as his mouth

drips open on the table.

Emily Brontë Has No Regrets

This phantom of expectancy. Who broke this?
Then called it fixed? Who named these things:
Heart, hope, life?
I did.

I named them from my own expectancy, named
Them so ferocious they formed from the fog of
Throat, tongue,
Spit.

I wanted decision's lurch to push life out of me
Fast, slick, through the belly of that expectancy –
Instinct, suckle
Grip

Carrying me while I carried it, out onto a moor
Of awful trees. So let's see wind do that thing
To trees, heaths.
Clefts

Of reason gone, the cliff sheared ever steeper
And the trees without shelter blasted into
Limbs like this.
Twist

And you are well-born, wind-blown, my own
Thing, my seedling, my foundling, my little
Lost lamb, my
Kid.

No nannies bleat for you. You are tough, almost
Dead. That tree points at you, through
Knuckles, fingers,
Wrists

Bent double back upon themselves. I must be
The author of this: you as some stiff-jointed
Flesh, wood, rock
Kissed

Out here to death. Where else could I have you?
There is not a colder, grander house of
Hall, roof, ruins
Than this.

Descent

You grew nervous of the chalk man's great prehistoric club.
I grew nervous of the strange cluster of hills around us oozing mist
and of the soil beneath my bare skin sniffing me out as a foreign body.
The trees in the valley below hunkered like old people gone beyond their sex
into archetype and the black cat that had followed us was suddenly, silently gone.
The sound of a car accelerating swung past our ears like the buzz of a lost bumblebee –
that small, that significant. We didn't make love, we rubbed each other up the wrong way,

Which was a sort of love, until the moon rose and we shivered back towards the car waiting
like a domestic pet kept well away from dragons. I was speechless with the stress of being
with you and have no clear memory left of stumbling on behind you as we went down,
except for the heart-skittering sound of a horse's iron hoof dropped onto a shed's
bare floor and how it rang like a warning bell before me, then behind me.
Nothing then except your beautiful back in the gloom until a lost drift
of music finally stopped you and when I reached you the troubled

question in your eyes was mine: were we under an enchantment, way down, beneath it all?

From a Lost Traveller's Diary

Even though
I am sick and can hear
the whistle of air through the
teeth of a bored snake I want to go
where the stone mouth of the god speaks
a root language; that is why I am travelling alone
under bellies of cloud dark with juice in spite of black
leopard yellow eyes and spiders waiting under contraptions
to pounce and paralyse. I want to feel a monk's tough hand pushing
my head into the tongue's curve, I want to feel the cool lick in there, the
whisper at the tip of my brain; I want to come back out into the sun with the first
symptom of a great infection: a rise at the back of my mind, gorge opening, fruit splitting
a gurgle of sound from my lips as I try to speak what the god said, when I was in his mouth.

The Village Says

Cows!
You are going right up my old spine this morning,
marching through me like a black and white surprise;
the same cow keeping close to the same haunch of
the cow in front, the same brown eye watching out,
the same thought in the heavy brain, the same milk
in the same udders, the same hooves beating on me.
Welcome back cows. I miss you now in these times
that are under the knife and stretched out to cover
new things. But you have reached the crossroads and
are turning away from me. Please send from the field
sometimes a faint echo of moo like a pied piper tune;
I'll know you are somewhere still green, a place not
quarried or buried in concrete; let a ribbon of your
scent drift down my street; and come back again, do,
for as you passed, the horses in the field by the bridge
danced, like children at the barriers watching a parade.

August 1976

Levels in reservoirs fall all through June
and July, while my mother's ankles swell.
The sky is a blue blaze. Curled in the kiln
I feel heat come through, I hear the bellows
of my mother's breath firing me up, so
warmth is all I can know or expect.
I am born hot, my bones well set, a row
of glazed gums seeded with teeth,
and a temper glowing red. The first day
is sunshine skeeting down bright corridors,
swinging off white skirts towards me as I lie
in the hot limbs and milk of my mother
swaddling me from head to toe, front and back,
as if she's guessed that if I cool, I crack.

Forecast

Storm surge is coming
but nobody knows
until it breaches the sea wall
and carries people from their beds.

There is no way to pass
this message on,
except in the cold fury of the
news itself, arriving on the hour

it has decided to break.

Mother's Guilt, 1986

The day she left the curling tongs plugged in
on the couch in the breakfast room, my mother
was wearing a bright pink skirt and top. While
the firemen pulled the charred couch to the garden
my sister and I stood awestruck
imagining the singed springs as our hair,
though all we had seen, when we came home
from school, was smoke with no sign of a flame.
The house still stood, only the cracked window
in the breakfast room showed the strain.
Until, that is, my mother came home from work
and stood in the black room, burning in her
bright clothes.   This made everything much worse:
watching her turn dangerous to the touch.

The Celibate

Religion, like red nails, keeps one hopeful
of something better just brushing at one's
fingertips, the gloss against the gloom, the
amazing opulence laid over deadened skin.

I paint my nails red, but keep them short so
I won't be called a trollop but will be
a sophisticate at prayer while dialling his
phone number, while brushing my hair, and

when I come up against his mighty chest,
my squoval nails (part square, part oval)
will pulse like little lanterns in his heart;
this is my career, this is my holy life.

Reunion

Persephone styles herself now as a tree
from which one leaf hangs and whose
bark is infused with a plutonic cool like
winter.
Nothing remains of her for her mother
who is blasted into shadow, stunned by
the thin slouch of her daughter who ate
only fruit

and plans to go under again, next year.

In Edinburgh

It all goes downhill in Mary King's Close.
The tenement's hope for a slice of sky
is bricked over by law courts to a tomb.
A plague of plastic rats squeaks around
the bird-beaked physician: both scare waxen
children stiff. Skin here fades faint as a block
pattern on old walls. At a blind window
a ghost girl sits, looking out at nothing.
Gardyloo! she sings and a sluice down to
the stink of the Nor Lough takes me with it,
but only as far as the lane's dead end
and dry wall. Life goes no further than this.
The door of the last house opens. The hall
leads to a room dark with arsenic paint

Up Above, Meanwhile

The wind hurries down the Royal Mile and
tartan rugs for sale in shop doorways break
into the swirl of a small skirmish for freedom.

Primary School Polling Station

Going in to cast my vote I pass a
large aquarium where a many-limbed
creature is splat on the glass. It hangs
over the plain fish of the tank that swim
past a sunken ship, bump their mouths on their
own reflections, then lazily retreat.   .
After voting, I go for a closer look
at this star drooling over such a wet world.
Not acting over eighteen at all,
I put my nose to the glass and see that
the undersides of the thing's tentacles
are lined with countless little suckers, some
of them waving, but most stuck to the task
of staying just exactly where they are.

Tongue Twister

You sucked my tongue so hard
it became a little less fixed in its socket,
a little more loose at the root.

After that, there was only one
thing I kept quiet, held back by a single
tendon. It snapped last night.

My tongue flew out, hit my hands
with a slap and lay there like a fortune-
telling fish. The way you

acted so surprised, as if it had
nothing to do with you, meant I didn't
have to wait for the fish to

twist and curl into a prediction of
red knots to know which way it would
end. You paused, then started

speaking - delicately, carefully -
and all I could hear was the click
of your tongue, infuriatingly intact.

Lost in the Gaeltacht

My radio is only picking up
button accordions and banjos.
Even the fields that wore walls like lace cuffs
are gone. I should have checked the map miles back.
Three cars coming at me like a posse
dazzle the road – I brake so close to the
drunk hitching for a lift that I can count
the threads of his quilted shirt, the whorls of
his thumb. I should have known this would happen:
even while RTE One was sinking
beneath the wavebands it was broadcasting
Irish poems and I had rolled down the
window, hoping that the stars' sharp crystal
might transmit a distant understanding.

(Above a gate in the walls around Galway was inscribed
'From the Fury of the O'Flahertys, Good Lord, Deliver Us'.)

From the Fury, Deliver Us

Salthill air-show does practice runs over
Galway, over the Corrib, over the
schoolyard where boys scramble to run riot
as jets coming low and fast contract in
to the hot circle of their boosters with
a huge thrust; diminishing dots that could
flatten the lot of us if they wished. The
Cathedral seems to know this: its green dome
is suddenly an eye with a blitz glint,
an endangered, defiant, skywards tilt.
Sarajevo past or Baghdad blast, this
any-town of happy streets could be starved
under siege and its people made endure
the taste of history in their own mouths.

Just then

a swallow dips, executes a perfect triple flip
and the silence streaming from its forked tail
loosens like a loop of cloud–smoke, and drifts.

River Scenes

I

The salmon is on the bank,
bright and stiff as a sword.
Then it jumps and the blade
tries to strike back into the
water but it bends, buckles.

II

A row of ducklings follow mother;
one is ringed around its chest with
a blue elastic band.
This mark of a strangulating death
singles out the unlucky ball of fluff
from the rest. Everyone
who watches its constricted paddle
up the canal feels the awful ripple
start to take effect.

III

A family of moorhens bob black on the water,
these quiet types who mostly keep to the reeds.
They look like a line of dot-dot-dots contained
within the parental bracket of two speech marks:
a flotilla shaped like an ellipsis, making me rest
like this

    '...
          '

for a moment on the bridge.

Art Exhibition

There is almost a whiff of seaweed, old
rope, gulls and stone from the paintings of gulls
on stone and seaweed wrapped up in old rope,
but not quite. I can smell the red wine and
the tang of the leather jacket on the man
next to me alright, and there is a waft
around me of somebody who could be
someone else. Leaving, I steal a wine glass
(the dark dots at the bottom like little
bloody clots) that is broken by the time
I get home. I wrap the sticky sharps up
in newspaper and put the stained glass
in the bin, all the time careful not to cut
myself and end up drawing the real thing.

First Words

Her punch raises a bump like Braille
into my pressed-down palm out here.

I form a round vowel of surprise;
kicks ripple across my fingers, pouring

something so close to understanding
across my hand I can almost grasp it.

But not yet. She has months of work
before I'll be able to say a word to her.

Still, it's a good beginning, this impact
on my skin: her signalled intention

to communicate, to penetrate,
                        I have somehow taken in.

The Occasion

On the occasion of her engagement
my sister gave me a gift of a diamond ring.

This makes no sense.

But she had been given the diamond ring as a gift
around the time of her engagement
(or possibly because of her engagement,
which would make no sense)

so she gave to me.

It fits my middle finger.

It's very small,
but it is a diamond and
it glitters. (At times it has been mistaken
for a surreptitious engagement ring

which could make sense, but is not the case).

What makes no sense, and what is the case
is that my sister gave me a diamond ring
on the occasion of her engagement
and it sits on my middle finger, glinting;
tiny, tiny diamond in a slender golden ring.

I have become nervous
that the jewel, smaller than a snow crystal,
will fall out and be lost, lost and unable to melt
away from this vast world of dust.

I have become attached to this ring
that signifies nothing,
except that there was no room on my sister's hands
for any more diamonds

and that
for whatever small beauty fell into them

my hands were free.

May

If I was to reconstruct your face, I would start
with memory
as my underlying base.

Anatomically foolish, but how else to recreate
that water-drop
hanging from your nose

and the hazel of your eyes? And if writing that
makes a witch of you
whose benign trinkets

I preserve, it is still a fair and proper likeness
because your shadow
while you stood beside me

stretched out next to mine on the village street,
crisp as if we flew
past the white, full moon.

Our Dead Grandmothers

Our dead grandmothers were women once
with armpits and groins
they had cramps, they opened their legs
they made their beds

Our dead grandmothers were women once
who stepped one foot after the other
into knickers that sat high on the waist
low on the legs

Our dead grandmothers were women once
who cupped their breasts into bras
bent their arms back, hooked the clasps
settled their shoulders under the straps

Our dead grandmothers were women once
with skin that grew its own perfume
to which they sometimes added more perfume
on the wrist above the pulse

Our dead grandmothers were women once
with moments of absence
when they closed their lips over a silence
no child's finger could un-seal

Our dead grandmothers were women once
who cared for the inherited hag,
turned her from withered side to side
with a twist of their own spines

Our dead grandmothers were women once
and we who are women now
will become in the dark, in the box
skeletons that are both female and unknown:

entire lives falling
              through a pelvic bone.

I am Listening

Someone keeps bumping things in the vestry.
The knocks and taps
come over the altar, under the vaulted dome
as if the building's very size
goes towards proving actions reverberate forever.

Listening is prayer for me this evening,
tiny aural shocks that re-teach the art of living.
I convince myself of the impossible,
believe I can hear the skinny wicks in the altar candles
take the flame held to them
by the man with the squeak in the soles of his shoes.
I sit and adore before the miniscule fizzle
that streaks into a smooth flame after three sizzles.

An old woman walks past
                    so soundless she's a miracle.

She lights a remembrance and puts a coin in the slot.

Up through the Cathedral
I can hear the pennies drop.